The End of the West

The End of the West
Michael Dickman

COPPER CANYON PRESS

PORT TOWNSEND, WASHINGTON

Cover art: Ralph Eugene Meatyard, *Untitled*, 1960. Gelatin-silver print, 7.5 X 7.25 inches. © The Estate of Ralph Eugene Meatyard, courtesy Fraenkel Gallery, San Francisco.

Copper Canyon Press is in residence at Fort Worden State Park in Port Townsend, Washington, under the auspices of Centrum. Centrum is a gathering place for artists and creative thinkers from around the world, students of all ages and backgrounds, and audiences seeking extraordinary cultural enrichment.

LIBRARY OF CONGRESS CATALOGING-IN-PUBLICATION DATA

Dickman, Michael, 1975–
  The end of the west / Michael Dickman.
      p. cm.
   ISBN 978-1-55659-289-8 (pbk. : alk. paper)
   I. Title.

PS3604.I299E53 2009
811'.6—dc22

                                        2008039990

98765432

COPPER CANYON PRESS

Post Office Box 271
Port Townsend, Washington 98368

www.coppercanyonpress.org

Acknowledgments

Thanks to the editors of the following journals, where some of these poems first appeared, sometimes in earlier versions: *The American Poetry Review, Field, Narrative Magazine, The New Yorker,* and *Tin House.*

✲

Thanks to the Michener Center for Writers, in Austin, Texas, the Vermont Studio Center in Johnson, Vermont, and the Fine Arts Work Center in Provincetown, Massachusetts.

✲

I wish to thank, for their loving-kindness and support of this work, my family: Wendy Dickman, Elizabeth Dickman, Matthew Dickman, Francis Cobb, the Castelluccis, Dana Huddleston, Darin Hull, and Ernie Casciato. And my friends: Carl Adamshick, Mike McGriff, Dorianne Laux, Joseph Millar, Meredith Martin, Major Jackson, Marie Howe, Tom Sleigh, Denis and Cindy Johnson, Lee Schore, Jerry Atkin, Charles Seluzicki, and the Christensen-Roberts household. Thanks to Franz Wright for his unfailing support and friendship.

Thank you Phoebe Nobles.

I love you Duke

for Pig

Contents

The End of the West

Nervous System

Make a list
of everything that's
ever been

on fire—

Abandoned cars
Trees
The sea

Your mother burned down to the skeleton

so she could come back, born back from her bed, and walk around the
house again, exhausted
in slippers

What else?

Your brain
Your eyes
Your lungs

*

When you look down
inside yourself
what is there?

You are a walking bag of surgical instruments
shining from the inside out

and that's just
today

Tomorrow it could be different

When I think of the childhood inside me I think of sunlight dying on
        a windowsill

The voices of my friends
in the sunlight

All of us running around
outside our
deaths

*

Someone is here
to see you
again

Someone has come a long way with their arms out in front of them
        like a child

walking down a hallway
at night

Make room for them—
they're very tired

I wish I could look down past the burning chandelier inside me

where the language begins
to end
and

down

Scary Parents

I didn't shoot heroin in the eighth grade because I was afraid of
            needles and still am

My friends couldn't
not do it—

Black tar
a leather belt
and sunlight

Scary parents

They filled holes
all afternoon
then we went to the movies

*

The shit-faced gods swam upstream inside them and threw wild parties

and stayed up
all night

Under their tongues
between their toes
their stomachs

All over their arms
wings

did not descend to wrap them up like babies

As promised

Still
there is a lot to pray to
on earth

*

Everyone is still alive
if not here then
someplace else

Climbing out of their arms

Resting their heads

On what?
No one is singing us
to sleep

Ian broke his mother's nose because she burned the pancakes

She left hypodermics
between the couch cushions
for us to sit on

Some of the Men

I had to walk around for a long time before I could see anything

The leaves
circling down the street
imitating the insides of seashells
imitating
my fingerprints

I could sense my father
sitting alone in his little white Le Car
staring off at the empty parking lot

No radio
No wind
No birds

Just some guy in his car looking out at the blacktop and the shadows
of telephone wires

It isn't a sad scene, not really

Some of us are getting
exactly what we asked for

Some of us
don't even have
to wait

*

Think of my grandfather, still drunk or asleep, passed out on top of my
       grandmother
       so she has to wait for him
       to come to

along with the late
Redwood City morning
the light skipping in
across

the swimming pool

The smell of failed sex
bourbon and
chlorine

Dead cigars

He taught me how to swim

with one of his hands beneath my legs and another beneath my stomach
how to cup my hands, how
to turn my head

Inhale and exhale
and move gracefully
through liquid

*

Look at
Josh's father—

Stumbling into the bedroom at three in the morning the two of us asleep
          and all that moonlight
          and beat his son's
          head against

the headboard

                    You fucker you fucker you asked for it

The moon

His jaw splashed across the pillowcase

*

The Parietal   Temporal   Occipital
The Atlas and Axis
Spheroid and

Spheroid

The real smile
real grin

Your movable and immovable joints

Your eyes
your orbits

Sutures

If given the chance
I would

break them all

*

For a long time my grandfather
tried to kill anyone
who came near him

Wives
Daughters
Stepdaughters

What is it called when insects are stuck forever in a kind of amber?

Then he got sick
and he was going to die anyway
and he stopped
trying to kill people

Then we could fall in love

*

My father's advice is claustrophobic and flat as it fills the soft leather
        booth inside the restaurant

Birthday lunch
Red neon
Cigarettes

What you need to do
is join the Army, the Marines
something

You need to be taught a lesson

*

Some of the men are standing in their backyards at night, looking up
        at the stars
            listening to the freeway

Their hands in their pockets

Everything's just
as it was

My hands
in my pockets, curled
into tiny
fists

My belt buckle

gleaming

Kings

Our crowns look nothing like his crown

needles and light and
needles *of* light
fingers
stamen

Our crowns are made of dead hair and get swept out with the trash
        or ripped out by hand

Our capes are bath towels
wrapped around our necks
and fastened with
giant safety pins

Not ermine, not
rabbits

I ran around the neighborhood playing King of the Block
in my red underwear

The trees didn't bow

I was not on fire
as he

passed by

*

None of my friends
are kings

anymore

They used to be good at being alive, pointing their index fingers at
        the trees, passing
        invisible sentences
        proclamations

knighting the birds
one by one

All down my street the new fathers
beat the kingness
out
of the
kings

when they came in for dinner
and when they
went to bed

The birds knocking against the windows
in the wind

and he wasn't in the wind

*

When I think of him now all alone
he looks like a mouse

King of the mice

He's white like we all thought
red eyes
red tongue
yellow teeth

Scampering across the kitchen floor in the middle of the night when
        we wake up
            and want to make a sandwich

Listen, when you turn back into nothing and disappear forever
down a hole in the floor
I want to go with you

But we can't go

What a motherfucker that is

The kitchen window
the only light
for blocks

Now we're going to know what it feels like

My Autopsy

There is a way
if we want
into everything

I'll eat the chicken carbonara and you eat the veal, the olives, the small
        and glowing
            loaves of bread

I'll eat the waiter, the waitress
floating through the candled dark in shiny black slacks
like water at night

The napkins, folded into paper boats, contain invisible Japanese poems

You eat the forks
all the knives, asleep and waiting
on the white tables

What do you love?

I love the way our teeth stay long after we're gone, hanging on despite
        worms or fire

I love our stomachs
turning over
the earth

*

There is a way
if we want
to stay, to leave

Both

My lungs are made out of smoke ash sunlight air
Particles of skin

The invisible floating universe of kisses rising up in a sequined helix
        of dust and cinnamon

Breathe in

Breathe out

I smoke
unfiltered Shepheard's Hotel cigarettes
from a green box, with a dog on the cover, I smoke them
here, and I'll smoke them

there

*

There is a way
if we want
out of drowning

I'm having
a Gimlet, a Caruso, a
Fallen Angel

A Manhattan, a Rattlesnake, a Rusty Nail, Stinger, Angel Face,
        Corpse Reviver

What are you having?

I'm buying
I'm buying for the house
I'm standing the round

Wake me
from the dash of lemon juice
the half measure of orange juice, apricot brandy
and the two fingers of gin
that make up paradise

*

There is a way
if we want
to untie ourselves

The shining organs that bind us can help us through the new dark

There are lots of stories about intestines

People have been forced to hold them, alive and shocked awake

The doctors removed M's smaller one and replaced it, the new bright
          plastic curled around
          the older brother

Birds drag them out of the dead and abandoned

Some people climb them into heaven

Others believe we live in one   God's intestine!

A conveyor belt of stars and saints

We tie and we loosen

minor
and forgettable
miracles

Returning to Church

Walking through the snow with her was enough, quiet enough, white
        breaking beneath
        our boots

White   then dirt
White

then concrete

Not a word

I watched the black branches of the oaks gliding above us
        like the shadows of koi

Shadows, she was singing
                    Shadows!

*

I had forgotten
all the promises they make
at church, singing
or

not singing—

A new body
A living water

I wanted to be very still and listen to her voice moving out in front of me

There are two houses

The dark and quiet
house of God
and the house of her

voice

*

The light through the stained-glass window was snow

Do you want to be home forever?
It's all right if you do

Kiss me in the pew among strangers who aren't strangers but His
        other homeless children

The light through the stained-glass window
was snow, not Grace
not Spirit

Not, lightly
His fingers

*

Everyone's so nice!

And they don't even know me, they don't think they have to, hand
        after hand
            they take my hand

A prayer of bone

The old, beautiful
Wurlitzer rising
behind us

It underwrites all our blessings, note for note, on its way up into the
        rafters

I don't have to explain

Hand after
hand

I don't have to be embarrassed

*

The black branches of the oaks glide above us like the shadows of koi

Disappearing
beneath leaves
and mud

What does God promise?

It's winter, so
the orange and red bellies of the fish
look like small fires

Soon everything will ice over

There won't be
any room, not
anymore

Little Prayer

The swing sets
covered in ice
are perfect statues
of moonlight

Buckets of snow

You can stand here all morning in darkness if you want to

There are monsters
hiding

all over the neighborhood

Maybe you are one

*

The snow comes down in feathered clumps, like someone pulling out
        their hair

Quietly

The street
The parked cars
The elms

Listen

don't let any of my dead friends come back

There they are
Walking up the street
dragged up the street
by their hair
by you

*

You think it's going to hurt, and it does, only not in the way that you
        imagined

Her hand there and then
not there
His
hand there
and then not
there

My little prayer:

Take
Take
Take

Me in a snow-white T-shirt and blue jeans
and you
in your

Heavy Crown

My Father Full of Light

Tonight the moths are beating the shit out of themselves against the
               screen door

It looks like smoke

So does the light
inside his rings, his
wristwatch

The blood swimming around inside his face
in lightning blotches beneath his skin
like the residue of beets
on a cutting board

also
emitted light

A blizzard of wings

*

He thinks God
is going to clean
everything up

Hands made from Light and Feathers, moving us around, dusting us off

Everything
settling back into the warm
colors of autumn
instead of getting
ground down
into glass

which, I get the feeling
diamond after
diamond
is what's really
going to happen

*

I could have
whatever I wanted
once a year

Whatever you want
it's on me

Coconut cream pies rotated slowly behind bright windows like the
          cities of heaven

The register sang
Flies collected
on our water glasses

My father, for a moment, was full of light

Men came and went

I knew

our waiter was the son
of someone

Late Meditation

What are you going to do?
Describe the light
falling

through the pitch pines
again?

Yesterday we put all our kids in the car, doused it with gasoline, and
        lit it on fire

Their eyelids
and toe-
nails

That was one day

The snow geese migrating above us in the dark was another

Wheeling

The light
is red
and

inextinguishable

*

Do you think His arms
are going to make
a cradle

for your head

so you can finally
fall asleep?

The yellow crocus just outside the front door is not a miracle of light

But pretty close
in its papery
stillness

The only color in the entire yard

We are trying
very hard

to be alone

*

One way
is to sit very still
and count
your breath

Another way
is to stare out the window
until your mind
disappears

The smell of the pine needles smoldering in the woods behind the
          lake is enough to return
          your mind

Needle by
needle

The doors were locked
from inside

Into the Earth

The best time was the first time, on the floor of her living room
        people walking past the apartment outside
        talking loudly

Almost naked
on the carpet
Finally!

If you take me
into the bedroom
you know
you could fuck me

Streetlight beginning to pile up outside her windows, along the
        couch, pooling into her
        sunken hips

White
Cathedrals

*

Your face is like everyone's
face underground
Tunneled

Pretty acre
after pretty acre

You aren't even here so I don't know why I'm telling you this except
        I'm telling myself
over and over again
by myself

You are not listening
with pity

*

The photos I took of the tide pools get close to the sand, the wind
            my hangover
            this morning

climbing over the rocks

They get close
but just fall short

They are a nice description of something beautiful that doesn't exist
            anymore

No one I loved had died for almost two years

Then Amy bled out
in a bathtub

Good Friday

I think the light
appearing, then
disappearing

across the trunk of the live oak
is the boss of everything

Not You

Not Your hands tearing up the grass in the neighbor's yard, fashioning
      little green crosses
        no one can fit on

We can put them to our lips though

and whistle

*

I don't see You everywhere
all night, and
I have all night

Fire ants walking the edge of a blade of grass in the moonlight

We'll want to keep our mouths
away from that one

A parade
all night, and I have
all night

Cords of wood stacked all over the neighborhood

Snakes asleep beneath the kindling

Stars—

Return, don't
return

*

The dogs bark
at something that never arrives
at my house

Why is that?

If You came back and it happened again
we would shave Your head
and attach black wires
to Your solar system
We would turn the dial
You would see Your mother
Your childhood
and small pockets
of darkness behind
Your eyes

turn to lightning

Someone would wipe You clean with a towel

Someone
would put You
in the ground

My Dead Friends Come Back

If you want to
come back, just you
I say it's fine

From the flattened universe
From His side
of the bed

Shave my head and put me in the ground with you surrounded by
        trillium

Trillium or
something else

Shit and violets

*

If you want to
come back, just you
I say it's fine

From endless singing
From the icy branches
of evergreens

I want to trade you sunlight for starlight, or star for star, the night sky
        disappearing for
        coffee in the morning

What I want

I want to fuck you again
on the living-room
floor

*

If you want to
come back, just you
I say it's fine

From your hijacked brain

From your skeleton
sparkling like change
on a countertop

Your life as light is just beginning in the cosmos, but you can come
            back if you want to

What a terrible place this is

Limping around
not in each other's arms
not like light
at all

Ode

When you cry like that you sound like meat being tenderized by
        hand

Beaten, flipped and
beaten again

If I'm deathly quiet
it's because I want to hear
the muscles flatten

The sun pours in from the other shore
and runs its fingertips
over the shank

Like a butcher in love!

Here—you can wipe
your hands
on my apron

*

It's not heaven
it's the early dark
Everything fighting
to be seen

Hands and
stars

Sometimes the bed seems to be made entirely of skin

Sheets of skin

Onion and Egyptian
my legs, your
stomach

Honey
I can't stop grinning

I'm having so much fun
trying to relax
around your fist

*

It's as if we're both standing on the wilder shore of some immaculate
        kitchen, our towels folded neatly, into bleached-
        white columns

I love your spine, chef

Serrated
Butterfly
Bird's Beak

I love
your technique

Lifting the veins up carefully in the early light and then putting them
        back down again

Lifting them up
Putting them back
Lifting them up

*

Do you think there's a difference
for the Lord
between

slow dancing in the kitchen at night, no music, your arms around my
        neck, and later

my face
in your ass?

I think His home is covered in dark leaves
cicada wings and
promises

a peaceful night
a perfect death

*

Are you hungry?
Do you want to get up?
Do you want some coffee?

I want to bow very low
all the way down to the ground
actually lie down
my face pressed hard
against the tiles
my arms out, and bow
to your fingers
your parents who put you here
your legs
the backs of your knees
your mouth
your chin
how you smell
how you smell at night
bow to your voice
across the kitchen
crooning

Come here
Come back
I'm going to bend you
over my knee

We Did Not Make Ourselves

We did not make ourselves is one thing
I keep singing into my hands
while falling
asleep

for just a second

before I have to get up and turn on all the lights in the house, one
        after the other, like opening
        an Advent calendar

My brain opening
the chemical miracles in my brain
switching on

I can hear

dogs barking
some trees
last stars

You think you'll be missed
It won't last long
I promise

*

I'm not dead but I am
standing very still
in the backyard
staring up at the maple
thirty years ago
a tiny kid waiting on the ground
alone in heaven
in the world
in white sneakers

I'm having a good time humming along to everything I can still
        remember back there

How we're born

Made to look up at everything we didn't make

We didn't
make grass, mosquitoes
or breast cancer

We didn't make yellow jackets

or sunlight

either

*

I didn't make my brain
but I'm helping
to finish it

Carefully stacking up everything I made next to everything I ruined
          in broad daylight in bright
                    brainlight

This morning I killed a fly
and didn't lie down
next to the body
as we're supposed to

We're supposed to

Soon I'm going to wake up

Dogs
Trees
Stars

There is only this world and this world

What a relief
created

over and over

Seeing Whales

You can go blind, waiting

Unbelievable quiet
except for their
soundings

Moving the sea around

Unbelievable quiet inside you, as they change
the face of water

The only other time I felt this still was watching Leif shoot up when
we were twelve

Sunlight all over his face

breaking
the surface of something
I couldn't see

You can wait your
whole life

*

The Himalayas are on the move, appearing and disappearing in the
        snow in the Himalayas

Mahler
begins to fill
the half-dead auditorium
giant step by
giant step

The Colorado
The Snake
The Salmon

My grandfather walks across the front porch
spotted with cancer, smoking
a black cigar

The whales fold themselves back and back inside the long hallways of
        salt

You have to stare back at the salt
the sliding mirrors
all day

just to see something
maybe

for the last time

*

By now they are asleep
some are asleep
on the bottom of the world
sucking the world in
and blowing it out
in wave-
lengths

Radiant ghosts

Leif laid his head back on a pillow and waited for all the blood inside him
        to flush down
        a hole

After seeing whales what do you see?

The hills behind the freeway

power lines

green, green
grass

the green sea

Marco Polo

My grandmother set sail on a small air mattress into the middle of
         the pool and fell asleep

Her fingers
dragging the water

The men talk quietly inside

The outdated
California architecture
dissolves

into pale greens, pinks
and stark
lemon

*

I want to set sail from the following three things:

My little sister, tied to her trundle bed, crying, forced to eat slices of
        orange
she believed were her goldfish

I tied her wrists
her feet

I did that

The neighbor kid I cornered, shouting   Say you're fat! Say it!
Say you're fucking fat!
and he said it

My mother

The waves out here
look like steel
baskets

*

My great-great-grandfather, my great-grandfather, my grandfather
     and my father
     all looking back
     over their shoulders

Half asleep in metal deck chairs

moving the ice around
in their drinks

Do you know who's going to kill you?

I'm going to kill you

*

Our limbs sound like sand poured out of a Venus Comb
Our brains tick like tidal pools

My grandmother

Our eyelids close like Golden Moons, Tiger Moons, Zebra Moons

My grandfather

Open and
close

*

At night
the voices on the patio
sound like small
darting birds

We set sail

The light
walks away from me
on the water

The light walks away from me
quickly

on the water

Wang Wei: Bamboo Grove

Alone

Finally

It's nice to sit in the bamboo dark
among the bamboo
dark

Guitars
and a low
whistle

I don't know anyone here!

Me and
the moon

One shining, the other
shining

*

It doesn't matter what I wanted

The air
in green waves

A park in the city
A bench
My friends

What I have
is finally invisible

Singing a little tune   *They can't take that away from me*

Look
the moon is up

The moon
is down

*

Do you think that's music
we're listening
to?

Ambulances
and dogs

The trees praying

Strangers walking their darlings beneath streetlights
whispering encouragement

Bending down
to scrape shit off the sidewalk
into little plastic bags

Sirens and
trees

All the music
that's left

*

You know
how we are going
to disappear

into the dirt forever

Or burn
into the sky
into oceans

Well, I love this about us
and I want to be able to do it
all by myself

It won't be scary
or cold

Not like what they told us at all

If there are spiders
and there will be
spiders

they will not kill us
in our
New Cities

The End of the West

1

My mother waits for me

breathing easily
having let her hair go
silver, white
longer now
shining

in this
one of her many
afterlives

The new world is black
and glassy

and looks like
the old world: pinpricked
by telephone poles
and stars

She's unbelievably patient

Her hair piled up
with long
metal needles
She's never been
this patient

Rocking back and forth
on an onyx-colored
front porch

Putting out cigarettes
and singing

She inhales
my shoulders
my legs

The many ways
I've lied to her

My tongue, how
I've tried to hurt her
My back, my
hands

She exhales my name

I want her to be happy

and that's why
she's here
My Annie Oakley

I want to be happy
and that's why

she's here

My Dale Evans

Her name
is a pair of pearl-handled
silver-inlaid
six-shooters

Everything she ever wished for
written in cursive
beneath
the barrel

Mom

There was no other life

She breathes in

Now
I remember

There were hundreds of
other lives
She chose
this one:

Childlight everywhere

Cutting across
the newly waxed
1975
linoleum

in the new kitchen: yellow
yellow
yellow

She breathes out

My mother dreams of being a child again
and also

of horses

cantering down the sidewalk
in lovely
California
light

The smell of lilacs
The sound of hooves
on concrete

She waves to us from on top of her pony
in chaps and a T-shirt

Little boots
Little hat
Little holster

A trick rider
playing to the crowd

At the age of five she's already waiting for me

But it's different

I was the crowd
My brother and sister
and me

In the rodeo delivery room

we clapped and
clapped

What is this like for her?

It's like when she and Mickey and Pat
would sneak up on the mares
at night

With belts

No saddles

Whispering their names

or the names
they'd give them

Buttercup
Mistletoe
Burnt Sienna

When I'm quiet enough
I can hear her
digging

the heels of her red-and-black
hand-stitched cowboy
boots
into the clay
around her

Calling me home
Over the range
Over the rhinestones
The stars
The six-shooters

Over the bluebottles

Over the bottle grass

The prairie

The promise

Rain
Birds
Horses
Spurs

2

My grandmother sips

Takes
another
sip

In her blue-light
cha-cha
afterlife
Are you thirsty?

Yes
I'm thirsty

Oh honey
this one is going
to last

Her tongue
edging the impossibly
thin stemware

A lake on fire

Gin Fizz
Tom Collins
swimming pools
wine spritzer

Gin Fizz
the Pacific Ocean
the Pacific Ocean at dusk
wine spritzer
lemon trees
Tom Collins
redwoods
Redwood City
a Baileys
a Baileys and coffee

The company of men

White Russian
Black Russian
White Russian

If she could play anyone
she'd play
Joan Crawford

If she could play opposite anyone
she'd pick Cary Grant

So handsome
in tails!

The Thrill Is Gone
Autumn Leaves
Look for the Silver Lining

Oh honey
Cheek to Cheek
I'm in heaven

In the movie she's misremembering
she's Joan
at the top of the stairs
in sequined
black

about to descend
on silver pumps

Backlit
by stars and
stardust

Grant waits at the bottom
carelessly turning
a silver cigarette case
over in his hands

His boyfriend waits for him
in the trailer outside

Her husband
waits for her in the bar

Stars and
stardust

Grant insists that they dance
at the foot
of the staircase

Despite the hour
Despite all the fake moonlight

His hand
flat against the flat of her back
so she has to move
where

he wants her to move

They look safe
and pretty

It's hard to see what Grant is wearing
because his hair is
so perfect

But the deathgown
my grandmother wears
is a silk-and-metal
design by

Edith Head

Tails and top hats
and black servants
that's for her

White canes and white ties
She throws rice and streamers
from the deck of a ship
headed south

She pulls the hem of her black-
and-white dress
into a Bentley

headed for the coast

Headed for the poolside
suburbs

Lemon trees
and blacked-out
bourbon

Her Cary Grant alcoholic husband
closing up
her

close-up

My grandmother sips

Takes another
sip
Blue light
Moonlight

Are you thirsty?

Yes
I'm thirsty

The veins in her hands look like jewelry

Her face
smiling looks like
credits rolling

3

My brother the Saint walks out among the trees

to cure them
of their blindness

To cure them

in his sacred
and feathered

afterlife

He listens carefully to the veins of the maple
pumping green

The metallic green
on the pin-
head

of a fruit fly

It smells like photosynthesis

Metal

A migraine

Saint Francis has nothing on my brother
walking the streets of Assisi
everywhere

Moving his hands
over the bark
and cancer

Making the sign, making the sign

Streetlights flicker

Ants gather
around his feet

In the burning miracle

The trees aren't really trees, the trees are really people
men women and children
we see that now

White sulfur
amputates their faces
leaving a clearing
made out of skin
and fever

My brother the Saint
steps from body
to burning
body

like an acrobat

Reopening the holes

Raising the dead of their mouths
Walking on the water
of their eyes

In the red miracle

He's a little tired
and full of
visions

Poppies in the snow

Blood in the toilet

He wants to take
and be
taken

He turns in his
red bed

our demons
into fleas, our hands
into stars

In the last miracle

my brother the Saint lifts the face off the west
like a handkerchief

Blue

with white curlicue designs
that look like
cotton
Lightly, lightly

He snaps it out into the wind
and lays it back down

smoothing out
the edges

hospital-tucking
the corners

4

Then I am found
walking around the old neighborhood
just like I never left

Trying to learn how to whistle

Watching the dogs
tear at the chain-link
fence

Back
for good

in my schoolyard
sidewalk, blacktop
afterlife
My friends waiting at the end of the street
to beat the shit out of me

one last
time

That's what I want, that
or I want to
fuck them

One or
the other

They're throwing rocks at the streetlights
sitting against
the curb

shooting heroin
getting blind and
calling

my name

I can hear my name
hanging

in the air

Not like an echo
like a moth

Furious in the
light

We won't be long
they keep
saying

We won't
keep you waiting

I want to tell you a story with my body

Look at my arms

What do they look like
from here?

Peonies

Can they look like peonies?

In this light, at this time
of day, dusk
nailing itself down
inside
the maple

My arms
blooming like peonies
slowly unfolding
into their tiny
colorful deaths

Heaven
is what you think it's going to be

What do you think
it's going to be?

White people in robes or
unending night

Whatever you want

It's yours

At the end of the street
a choir of trees
lines up

in perfect silence

They don't say my name
but my name
is out there

When the springtime comes again
there won't be anything left
but ash

beneath our fingernails

collecting
on the tops of our eyelids
in the pools of our
eyes

My tongue
asleep in ash, my teeth
beginning to sparkle

That's before
we start turning into shit

before You

I want to say that there's something
missing
from heaven

and I think
it's the whisper
of bodies

Trees
Water
Light

We won't do this
again

Listen to those stitches
splitting open
in the air
above me

leaving stars
in a dark
I can hardly plot my way through

Float like a butterfly

Sting like a bee

My muscles latch and unlatch
with little clicks
opening

like a door
into Your house

You had this shit coming, they whisper
from the corner

You're going to be sorry

About the Author

Michael Dickman was born and raised in Portland, Oregon.

LANNAN LITERARY SELECTIONS

For two decades Lannan Foundation has supported the publication and distribution of exceptional literary works. Copper Canyon Press gratefully acknowledges their support.

LANNAN LITERARY SELECTIONS 2009

Michael Dickman, *The End of the West*

James Galvin, *As Is*

Heather McHugh, *Upgraded to Serious*

Lucia Perillo, *Inseminating the Elephant*

Connie Wanek, *On Speaking Terms*

RECENT LANNAN LITERARY SELECTIONS FROM COPPER CANYON PRESS

Lars Gustafsson, *A Time in Xanadu*, translated by John Irons

David Huerta, *Before Saying Any of the Great Words: Selected Poems*, translated by Mark Schafer

June Jordan, *Directed by Desire: The Collected Poems*

Sarah Lindsay, *Twigs and Knucklebones*

W.S. Merwin, *Migration: New & Selected Poems*

Valzhyna Mort, *Factory of Tears*, translated by Franz Wright and Elizabeth Oehlkers Wright

Taha Muhammad Ali, *So What: New & Selected Poems, 1971–2005*, translated by Peter Cole, Yahya Hijazi, and Gabriel Levin

Dennis O'Driscoll, *Reality Check*

Kenneth Rexroth, *The Complete Poems of Kenneth Rexroth*

Ruth Stone, *In the Next Galaxy*

C.D. Wright, *One Big Self: An Investigation*

Matthew Zapruder, *The Pajamaist*

For a complete list of Lannan Literary Selections from Copper Canyon Press, please visit Partners on our Web site:

www.coppercanyonpress.org

The Chinese character for poetry is made up of two parts: "word" and "temple." It also serves as pressmark for Copper Canyon Press.

Since 1972, Copper Canyon Press has fostered the work of emerging, established, and world-renowned poets for an expanding audience. The Press thrives with the generous patronage of readers, writers, booksellers, librarians, teachers, students, and funders—everyone who shares the belief that poetry is vital to language and living.

Major funding has been provided by:

Anonymous (2)

Beroz Ferrell & The Point, LLC

Cynthia Hartwig and Tom Booster

Lannan Foundation

National Endowment for the Arts

Cynthia Lovelace Sears and Frank Buxton

Washington State Arts Commission

For information and catalogs:
COPPER CANYON PRESS
Post Office Box 271
Port Townsend, Washington 98368
360-385-4925
www.coppercanyonpress.org

This book was designed and typeset by Phil Kovacevich. The text is set in New Caledonia, a digital version of Caledonia, a transitional serif typeface designed by William Addison Dwiggins in 1938 for the Mergenthaler Linotype Company. The headings are set in Clarendon, an English slab-serif typeface that was created by Robert Besley for the Fann Street Foundry in 1845. Printed on archival-quality paper at McNaughton & Gunn, Inc.